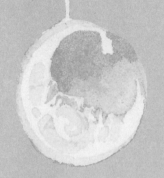

Reach
for the Moon

Stories and poems by
Samantha Abeel

Watercolors by
Charles R. Murphy

Edited by Roberta Williams

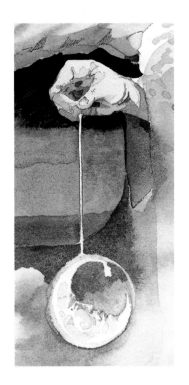

Pfeifer-Hamilton
Duluth Minnesota

Pfeifer-Hamilton Publishers
210 West Michigan
Duluth, MN 55812   218-727-0500

Reach for the Moon

The following publishers have given permission to use material from copyrighted works: From *Brush Calligraphy* by Arthur Baker. Reprinted by permission of Dover Publications.

The following persons generously allowed photographs of paintings from their collections to be used in the book: Barbara and Michael Dennos, John and Katherine Williams, Darryl and Gerrie Milarch, David and Roberta Williams, Delores Gilbert Pike, Carolyn Lawrence Geer, Kenneth and Jocelyn Lesperance, and Arlene and Doug Frantz.

Printed in the United States of America by Horowitz/Rae Book Manufacturers, Inc.
10   9   8   7   6   5   4   3

Editorial Director: Susan Gustafson
Art Director: Joy Morgan Dey

Library of Congress Cataloging-in-Publication Data
Abeel, Samantha, 1977-
    [What once was white]
    Reach for the moon / stories and poems by Samantha Abeel ; watercolors by Charles R. Murphy ; edited by Roberta Williams.
       p   cm.
    Originally published: What once was white. 1st ed. Traverse City, Mich. : Hidden Bay Pub, c1993.
    Summary: Poetry, written by a girl with learning disabilities, reflects her feelings and experiences.
    ISBN 1-57025-013-8 : $17.95
    1. Children's writings, American. 2. Learning disabilities—Literary collections. [1. Learning disabilities—Literary collections. 2. American poetry. 3. Children's writings, 1946- . III. Title.
[PS3551.B334W48 1994]
811' .54—dc20
93-46417

Dedicated to all those who daily struggle with difficulties and to those who endeavor to help them. Also to my parents, David and Elizabeth Abeel, who have given me unconditional love and the strength to never give up. To all those who supported this project, thank you for helping us reach for the moon.

Samantha's Story

A TREE that stands in the moonlight reflects the light, yet also casts a shadow. People are the same. They have gifts that let them shine, yet they also have disabilities, shadows that obscure the light. When I started this project in the seventh grade, I had trouble telling time, counting money, remembering even the simplest of addition and subtraction problems. Yet no matter how hard it was to stay afloat in this ocean of troubles, there was something inside of me, something that became my life preserver—and that was writing.

SEVENTH GRADE was a horrible year. I hated school. Every night I would come home and kiss the floor and revel that I had made it through one more day without totally messing up, or if I had, at least I was still alive. Then I would remember that I had to go back the next day and brave through all the same trials. With that thought, the tears and panic attacks grew. Yet one hour of my day was a refuge. Here, there weren't any concepts with numbers, measurements, algebra, or failure. It was my seventh-grade writing class. I had begun to experiment with creative writing in sixth grade, but in seventh grade I discovered how much writing was a part of me and I was a part of it.

TO BUILD on this, my mother asked Mrs. Williams, who was my English teacher, if she would work with me by giving me writing assignments and critiquing them as a way of focusing on what was right with me and not on

what was wrong. Charles Murphy, a family friend, lent us slides and pictures of his beautiful watercolors. I began to write using his images as inspiration. I discovered that by crawling inside and becoming what I wrote, it made my writing and ideas more powerful.

IN EIGHTH GRADE I was finally recognized as learning disabled. I was taken from my seventh grade algebra class, where I was totally lost and placed in a special education resource classroom. Special education changed my life. It was the best thing that ever happened to me. I could raise my hand in that class, even when being taught the most elementary concepts, and say, "I don't get it." It was the most wonderful feeling in the world. Eighth grade was my best year at the junior high. It is an illusion that students in special education have no abilities. Special education just means that you learn differently. I am so thankful for specially trained teachers who have been able to help me and many other kids like me.

IF YOU STRUGGLE with a disability, the first thing you need to do is find something that you are good at, whether it's singing or skate boarding, an interest in science or acting, even just being good with people. Then do something with that. If you are good with people, then volunteer at a nursing home or at a day care center; if you love skate boarding, work toward a competition. If it's singing, join a school choir. Even if you can't read music (like me) or read a script, you can always find ways of coping and compensating.

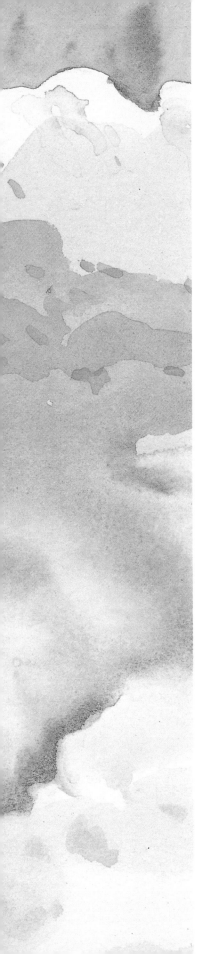

NEVER LET your disability stop you from doing what you are good at or want to do. I have trouble spelling and I'm horrible at grammar, but I was lucky enough to have teachers who graded me on the content of what I had to say instead of how bad my spelling and punctuation were. I was able to use a computer to compensate.

REMEMBER that if you have trouble in school, it might not be because you don't fit the school, it might be because the school doesn't fit you. Be an advocate for yourself. Keep trying. You may not fit in now, but whether you're seven or seventy, one day you will find a place where you excel.

AT THE BEGINNING of ninth grade we realized that what had started out as an art/poetry project had grown into something more. Because getting the right teachers and having the right educational placement made such a difference in my life, we realized it was a message we wanted to share. LD does not mean "lazy and dumb." It just means you have another way of looking at the world. I hope through my writing and what we have all contributed to this book to remind people that if you're standing in the shadow of the tree, you may need to walk to the other side to see the light it reflects. They are both part of the same tree; both need to be recognized and understood. This is my reflection of the light. Welcome to my book.

—SAMANTHA ABEEL

Self Portrait

To show you who I am
I crawled inside a tree, became its roots, bark and leaves,
listened to its whispers in the wind.
When fall came and painted the leaves red and gold
I wanted to shake them across your lawn
to transform the grass into a quilt, a gift spread at your feet,
but their numbers eluded me,
so I turned a piece of paper into my soul
to send to you so that you might see
how easily it can be crumpled and flattened out again.
I wanted you to see my resilience,
but I wasn't sure how to arrange the numbers in your address,
so I danced with the Indians in the forest
and collected the feathers that fell from the eagle's wings,
each one a wish for my future,
but I lost track of their numbers, gathered too many,
and was unable to carry them home
so I reaped the wind with my hair,
relived its journey through my senses, and
felt its whispered loneliness, like lakes in winter,
but it was too far and you could not follow me.

Now I've written out their shadows
like the wind collects its secrets
to whisper into receptive ears, and I
will leave them at your doorstep,
a reminder of what others cannot see,
a reminder of what I can and cannot be.

Wellspring

If you want to fill the well, make a boat out of paper,
set it on a dry, and dusty river bed,
cracked and wrinkled like the face of a grandmother.
Lie down on its fragile planks,
spread your hair over the edge like ivy
to cling to the broken sand.

Let your thoughts begin to trickle
as if they were rain,
soaking your clothes and hair
until you feel yourself begin to drift along
on the current of ideas
like a leaf fallen on a river.

Spinning across reflections of the sky
and eddying through the willows,
find the current below you,
seeking its way into the ancient stone edifice of the well,
pouring into its empty circle
just as love pours into an empty heart.

The well becomes full
and your words are lifted in a bucket—
brought into the sunlight
where the thirsty dip their hands in and drink.

 What Once Was White

Emptiness no longer prevails, her song has now begun.

The harmony calls forth images,

and as she weaves her melodic tune,

his brush keeps frantic time;

Sweeping the canvas, each note becomes a swirling color.

What once was white is transformed,

and a new world flows forth.

Silver notes become strands of her hair,

entwining fish which wave and weave among the brush strokes.

Butterfly wings emerge from the treble clef,

painting jewels upon her robe which shimmer like wet paint.

A noble oak springs from the bass clef

reaching in supplication for the tip of the brush

The canvas becomes a place where songs are pictures

and pictures are symphonies;

Harmony and color combine,

creating windows to a life within a life;

Immortality swells with each note.

Sunrise

Silently in the darkness
pale and hushed
I dream about this still cold world.
Opening my eyes,
waiting to part the curtain of night,
I ascend,
and the grass, once black, is green—
stretching toward the sky.
The wind yawns through the trees,
and I gently caress the darkness from their leaves
and whisper "Wake."
The birds take flight
carrying my light upon their wings.
I behold this newly born world
and whisper in the ears of those who
covet darkness,
"You can't keep out the light."

Alone

There is a place where we all go
when we must sit alone:
A place where the birds are free to fly,
A place where the sun and its flowers bow in shadow,
A place where the fog is like a veil
and everything is protected,
A place where our souls are set free
and we are allowed to play our own song.

Quilt

In the sun, my grandmother would sit,
calico and gingham spread long,
like a river speckled in fall leaves,
over her skirt.
Slowly gathering the pieces,
bringing them all together
she would rock, needle in hand.
"Life is a quilt made of many different
faces,"
she used to say,
"a fabric
of different goals and dreams,
each with different colors,
different eyes,
different hands,
yet bound together by a single piece of thread."

Come All the Old

While the ocean above me uncovered its pearl and the village ceased its bustle and quieted under that spell called sleep, I looked out from my window to the street below. All was still and unmoving except for the moonlight that tripped over the cobbled stones as if it were a child at play. Like a figure in a dream, a man came walking down the street and as he stepped into the moonlight, I could see his face. His eyes were shaped like the sun as it sets below the sea. His face was rough and unshaven, like a field just after harvest. He looked old, but I couldn't tell how old. Upon his back he carried a cage full of chickens and birds, and on his head was an old lamp shade with several feathers jutting like blades of tall grass.

Stopping at the corner, he slowly removed the cage from his back and opened its little door. Bowing as if before a king, the old man watched each bird flutter onto the pavement. Silently he took from his sack a worn set of bagpipes. Gingerly placing the mouthpiece to his thin lips, he began to play. At first, the notes seemed to wheeze, but soon they cleared and the bagpipe music danced before him down the street. Limply,

an old bag woman hobbled by, causing the birds to flutter as she passed.

Suddenly, as if her head had been attached to a string, she raised it and after staring at the strange old man for a minute, she began to dance, sending the birds scattering. When the old man saw this, he began to play more rapidly and his music seemed to say, "Come all who have suffered, who have seen history's face, those who have been forgotten or for whom death is on its way. If life has done you good, then dance for joy. Come all the old and be young again."

One by one the old people of the village arrived, lured by the sound of the music. Men who hadn't walked in years threw down their crutches, and women whose backs were bent by time were straightened. People who had been lying on their death beds were suddenly alive and full of energy. They danced among the birds, sending feathers flying. The old man led them down the cobbled street and into the darkness beyond, yet his music seemed to linger in the moonlight and whisper, "Come all the old and be young again."

Leaves in the Fall

They are the leaves in the fall,
the snow on the ground.
They are the wind in the trees,
the waves upon the sea.
They were our hopes and our dreams,
yet now their chairs are left empty,
their books unopened.

At first we did not notice the empty chairs,
or the unread stories.
We wanted to forget them,
like a child wants to forget his nightmares.
Now we realize our mistakes,
for they were heroes,
and we should honor them for what they gave,
and what they gave up.
A human life is a gift
more precious than anything,
and it should never be wasted.

We cannot just forget that they are no longer here,
that their voices will no longer be heard,
their smiles no longer seen.
We cannot just forget that they will never feel the sun
or count the stars,
for they were a part of us,
a part of our country.
They are the leaves in the fall,
the snow on the ground.
They are the dead of Viet Nam.

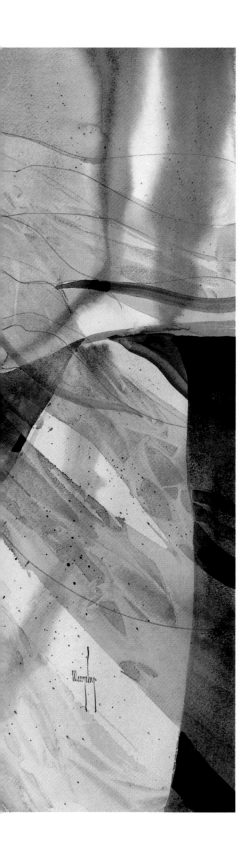

Voices of Ancestry

Voices in the canyon wind have uncovered my
deaf ears—
kind
pleading
strong
searching
wistful
caring
frightened
voices—
whispers of what used to be
before my ancestors left this canyon,
before they bled into the sea
and were lost.

Shivers in the Blackness

The lake is still, and the trees stand silent for each has become a shadow. An eagle takes flight, his wings riding upon the promises of the past. From this darkness, his cry is picked up by the wind and taken to an ancient land. There, in the night, a hand is stretched out beckoning the eagle who appears from the darkness. It is the hand of a woman who comes with the night to hear the words that are spoken by the wind. In the dawn she will give them to her people. The eagle cries, and the whispers begin. They are sighs as they pass her cheek, turning into words and filling her ear. After they are spoken, they drift off among the strands of her hair and die. The words of the wind that are spoken this night are few, but full of truth. "Listen to the wisdom echoing from deep within your memories. Though it is hidden, it is always there. Feel for it through the darkness." The whispers then fade, and the eagle spreads his wings to the dawn. As he disappears into the darkness of the future, a feather floats from the sky to land gently upon the surface of the lake, sending shivers through the blackness.

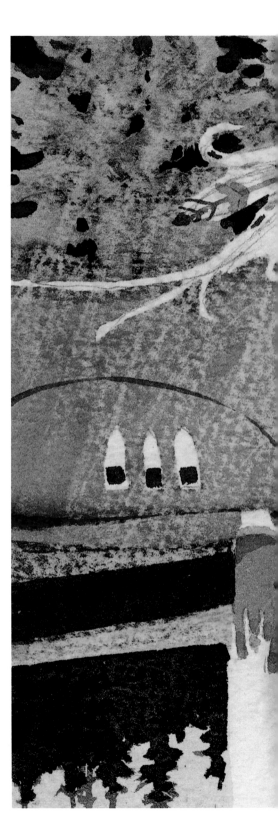

Music of the Heart

Like shadows dancing in the light of a flickering candle, the waves rose from the mist, each one a ghost, gray and cold, trying desperately to touch the warmth of life. Yet just as its icy fingertips were about to claim victory, they were pulled back into the mist, back into the cold and gray, where they were forced to wait in the shadows until they were allowed to rise again.

Silently, my eyes scanned the curtain of mist looming about me; above, the fall sky was a dull gray. I sat down upon a tall and weathered rock, and I could see by its deep cracks that the lake had already scrolled out its name upon its rounded surface. Slowly, I bent down and picked up a feather that was lying next to me. I lifted it above my head and released it into the air. Silently, I watched as it spun upon the breeze and gently landed in the sand. It was then that I heard it, like a gentle whisper of a lullaby. It filled my ears. It was a violin song that seemed to be played by the wind. At first it sounded distant, but before I knew it, it was upon me, and I could feel its every note run like a river through my mind. I felt a gust upon my face. I turned, and there, sitting before me, was an old man, his face gathered in wrinkles and his hair hanging about him like cobwebs.

Slowly, he raised his black eyes to me. They were deep, almost never-ending, and within them I knew there was a message hiding in the darkness, but it seemed as if something prevented me from discovering it. In his hand he held a violin. "I knew you would come," he said in a voice like a spring breeze.

"Who are you?" I asked. "What do you mean, you knew I would . . ."

"Hush, hush, child," he said interrupting me. "I cannot hear the music when you talk!"

"What music?" I asked. "What are you talking about?"

"Why, the music being played by the waves. Now hush so I can listen."

We sat for a moment in total silence, then he picked up his violin and began to play. It was a song like no other, each note seeming to cry and to laugh, and with each emotion I was taken with it. After he finished, he began to smile. "Why do you not smile?" he asked. "Do you not hear? It is a joyful song!"

"What song?" I asked in confusion. "All I heard was your violin."

"My dear," he said, "forgive me. I did not know you were deaf, but I shall soon fix that." Vigorously he set his violin to his shoulder and began to play.

Like the spires of a steeple, the masts of long dead ships began to rise from their sandy graves below the lake and shoot up from the mist. Most of them were nothing but scattered pieces of wood, a few sails covering them like torrents of wet leaves. I felt myself begin to shake; everything was spinning, then all went black.

I must have fainted, for when I awoke, I was lying on the deck of a ship whose wood was well worn and whose mast was crying out like a raven. Slowly, I got up and went to the ship's railing. We were moving quickly, cutting through the waves like a knife. No land was in sight. It was then that I noticed a gaping hole in the ship's hull, and that there was but one sail ripped through the middle. Just then I heard a voice that seemed to creep up behind me, and with it a low, nearly inaudible violin song, "So you have awakened."

It was the voice of the old man.

"Why have you brought me here?" I asked, growing angry. "What do you want from me?"

His black eyes looked into mine, searching. "My child, when I play the violin, I play it for the waves on the lake, for the gulls crying up above, and for those who have learned to listen with their heart and not their ears. For the ears only pick up the sounds from the surface, and not what is waiting beyond. You see, everything in life has a harmony, an ever-flowing song. For the moment, it is my music that keeps us afloat upon the coldness swirling below. Yet, my music cannot go on forever." He stopped playing. The whole ship lurched forward and I could hear the bottom begin to fill with water. "That is why you must learn to hear the eternal music of the heart and let it keep you afloat."

Just then the rain began to fall upon us and the waves grew high, moaning, reaching, grabbing at my ankles, trying to pull me down to their home below. "Keep playing!" I exclaimed. "We shall sink if you don't!" The old man just stood there, now barely visible through the driving rain and wind. "Are you crazy?" I yelled. "Keep playing!" I could feel the water. It was now to my waist and nothing but the mast of the ship rose above the waves. I moved toward it and grabbing hold, I felt myself sink with it.

The water rose to my ears, flooding them. My hand reached up to the sky, hoping to grab hold of the invisible when I heard it. The music of my heart. It rushed through me like the tide. Suddenly, the sky cleared, and I could feel the warmth of the sun upon me. The water became a glorious blue as the gray dissipated. I felt myself being lifted and carried upon the waves, their wrath now settled. Gently, I was set upon the rock. Next to me lay the feather. The mist had disappeared and I could hear the music, not with my ears, but with my heart.

If You Want to See

If you want to see the past,
look around you
for everything you do is
living out the legacy of those
who came before you . . .

Feathers, the open plain
a life following
the heartbeat of a drum.
Peace. Simplicity.
The eyes of a people
looking with hope,
to the future.

If you want to see the present,
look around you
for it is what you are building
for those who will come
after you . . .

Poverty, not enough room,
the dreams have ended.
Feathers float to the ground, and
drums no longer beat their rhythm.
The eyes of a people
look on with misgiving
to the future.

If you want to see the future,
look inside you
for it is where all the building
begins.

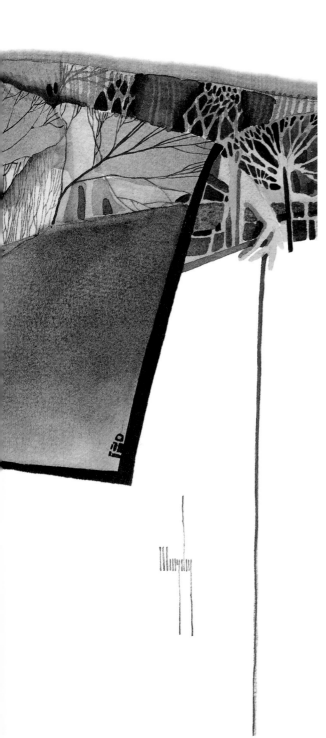

The Cloak

I am old, the sun has set,

it is time for me to fade into the background of life;

Death has given me his cloak to wear.

Do not worry, for his cloak is warm, and the chill north

wind can no longer harm me.

I can feel my soul as it is pulled from me and

taken to a place where it can be at

peace forever.

It is time. My breath becomes the falling

breeze, and my body the solid

stem; my arms become the branches

reaching to a higher grace, and my

hair unfolds into leaves of light.

I have entered the forest of

eternity and stand as a tree should.

A sigh passes from my lips,

and all is still.

I am old,

and the sun

has set.

Drawing the Curtain of Night

Crumple the day, shred the sunlight and
scatter it into the sky
Summon clouds, shape into an alabaster mountain, then
sculpt his benign and powerful features.

Watch as with one hand he grasps the curtain of night,
drawing darkness over the edge of the earth.
In the hush, the world becomes still
waiting expectantly for the moon to kindle the sky.

Carefully, he suspends it amongst the stars
then stands back, appraising his work
before disappearing behind the curtain to
wait for the whisper of sunlight.

Samantha's Journey

. . . this very
bright child was in
very big trouble

Nurturing the gifts within

As early as first grade, the child we knew as bright and imaginative was coming home scared and unhappy.

One evening during my daughter's second-grade year, a simple flash card, 5–3=2, changed our lives. Her teacher had told us that Samantha seemed to need a little extra help in basic math. Now, working with her, I realized that my bright, verbally agile child had no concept of the meaning of 5, of 3, of 2. As a result of my frustration at trying to "make her see," we were both in tears.

We had been confident that she would be a successful student. She had shown a precocious curiosity and an amazing talent for memorization. But during kindergarten Samantha became very quiet and observant; and as early as first grade, the child we knew as bright and imaginative was coming home scared and unhappy.

With the flash card episode, I knew something wasn't working right in Samantha's learning. Eager to know what could be done, I asked the school for help. They referred me to the Individualized Educational Planning Committee, or IEPC, a group of teachers, psychologists, counselors, and parents that evaluates children with suspected learning disabilities.

The evaluation revealed a large disparity in skills. Samantha combined strength in her language and thought patterns with total confusion in numbers. The IEPC recommended, however, that to protect her self-esteem she not be pulled out of her classroom for special help. "She is so bright, she'll be fine," they told us. "Be glad it's not a problem with reading. She can always use a calculator."

Samantha's happiest math experience came in third grade, the year of multiplication tables. Her uncanny ability to memorize made her a star. Everyone cheered her success, and I naively thought her problems were solved.

Fourth, fifth, and sixth grades brought different stories. She simply could not keep up with the new concepts, even with the help of a wonderful tutor. Coupled with her inability to perceive numerals as anything but oddly shaped symbols was an inability to tell time, count money, or spell. She knew that even though her grades were good, she wasn't really "getting" it.

During seventh grade, as the increasing stress

As well as getting the special help she needed, Samantha was allowed to join an advanced creative writing class. She finally had balance in her life, with both her strengths and her weaknesses being tended to.

Samantha faced began to cause panic attacks, we became determined to find help for her. She had to be identified as learning disabled to qualify for a specially trained teacher in math. We went back to the school, this time armed with more information and more confidence that we knew Samantha and her abilities best. We insisted that she be tested and retested until an accurate assessment finally was made. Enlisting the help of the learning disabilities teacher, the general math teacher, and the school guidance counselor, we finally got the help Samantha needed—but not without controversy. Many people have difficulty grasping the concept that a child can be both gifted and learning disabled.

Today, Samantha provides a wonderful example of what can happen when parents listen to their children, schools listen to parents, and they all work as a team. As well as getting the special help she needed, Samantha was allowed to join an advanced creative writing class. She finally had balance in her life, with both her strengths and her weaknesses being tended to. As a result, her symptoms of stress disappeared.

Learning disabilities do not go away. Samantha, and other children like her, will always face challenges. But with the help of the adults in their lives, they can gain coping strategies to make the challenges conquerable.

Parents and teachers must learn as much as possible and be persistent when the answers don't fit the questions. Help comes in many forms: books, organizations such as the Learning Disabilities Association (LDA) and the Orton Dyslexia Society, and networks of parents and educators.

A child is not the sum of the results of standardized tests. Each one, whether he or she has a learning disability or not, has a special gift of some kind. If we encourage and nurture the child, believe in the gift, and support learning in whatever way necessary, we'll have more stories like Samantha's.

—ELIZABETH ABEEL

Finding the key to learning

When we look for possibilities and potential in every student, then nurture those qualities, all children become successful learners.

Have you ever received an unexpected gift? One that not only surprised but changed you? I have, though at the time I didn't recognize it.

Samantha entered my seventh-grade classroom in 1990 as a quiet, shy girl. It didn't take long, however, for her to introduce herself in a compelling way: she wrote. She brought to her assignments insight beyond her years, and her writing showed a gift for imagery and language.

Despite this agility with words and capacity for insight, Samantha struggled with spelling, verb tenses, word omissions, and other technical problems. I learned that these difficulties were insignificant compared to her experience with math. As I got to know her better, I realized that in my classroom, where she excelled, she became a different child from the one who was completely intimidated in her math class. I was determined that my classroom would continue to be a place where Samantha succeeded.

To help with spelling, she used a word processor with a spell-checker. I ignored left-out words and mechanical errors and was flexible about due dates when her school assignments overwhelmed her. These adaptations were a small price to pay for the writing she could produce.

Slowly, Samantha's confidence grew and she bloomed. At the end of the school year, we didn't want to lose our momentum. Her mother, who had come to see Samantha's writing as a lifeline, called me with an interesting proposal. Would I be willing to give Samantha writing lessons?

We chose to structure the summer's writing around the work of an artist we all admired. Charles Murphy knew what it was like to be different, to be constantly discouraged. In high school, he had been denied the chance to take art classes; art wasn't on the college preparatory track. He was eager to encourage Samantha because he empathized with her struggle to pursue what she did well, against great odds.

When we started the project, Samantha had never written poetry, but her imagery-rich language seemed perfect for that medium. We went through boxes of slides of Charles's work and visited gallery openings and shows to see his paintings up close. Insights and images poured from Samantha. She was finally free to express what had been locked inside.

The first time we shared Samantha's writing with Charles, we nervously wondered if she'd got it "right," if what she saw was justified by his own perceptions of his work. Both of these remarkable people deserve praise: Samantha for being courageous enough to share her inner world and Charles for accepting her work seriously, critically, as artist to artist. The poems were a success in every way.

I suspect that many more Samanthas sit in our classrooms: the quiet ones who hide out in the back, the ones who always "forget" their homework or constantly apologize, the ones who cover up by distracting us with their behavior, their language, or their attitude. How many have we missed because we didn't have the right key, didn't know a key existed, didn't even know the door was locked?

I hope Samantha's story provides inspiration for those who are struggling to contend with their disabilities, and also serves as a reminder to educators everywhere. When we look for possibilities and potential in every student, then nurture those qualities, all children become successful learners. The willingness to help them should define the word "teacher."

—ROBERTA WILLIAMS
TRAVERSE CITY WEST JUNIOR HIGH SCHOOL

To a Special Teacher

When the sun rose
from under its misty veil,
you were there to watch,
like the birds over the sea.
When the wind came quietly
and rested in your ear,
you listened, as the earth would at dawn.
When the rain fell,
you reached out with your hands
and let it wash everything away,
like waves as they grasp the shore.
When the plain brown seed was planted,
you could already smell the fragrance of
the flower that was to come,
and you were proud
as a good gardener should be.

Thank you for believing
that there was a flower waiting inside
and for taking the time
to help
and watch it grow.
When the sun rose
from under its misty veil,
you were there to watch,
and I am thankful.

Samantha

Searching for help

Each child, each circumstance is unique, and there is no one correct path to follow. However, the following suggestions may serve as a basic road map if you suspect that your child has a learning problem:

- Talk to your child's teacher. Express your concern.
- Consider having your child evaluated by the school district or a community clinic.
- Think of the school system as a resource center and learn all you can about the services it can or cannot provide.
- Consult with your state and local offices and organizations for the learning disabled.
- Learn all you can about the nature of your child's learning difference and become an informed advocate for your child.
- Believe in your observations and feelings; you know your child best.
- Be your child's parent. It's usually best for someone else to act as tutor.
- Be tenacious in supporting your child. Persistence may be your greatest asset.

- Most importantly, listen to your child. Express your confidence, and vigorously support your child's efforts to find things that he or she is good at, demonstrating through your words and actions that you really care.

The organizations listed below can be very helpful for those with learning disabilities. Consult the national organization for the address of your state or local chapter:

Learning Disabilities Association of America
4156 Library Road
Pittsburgh, PA 15234

Orton Dyslexia Society
Suite 382 Chester Building
8600 LaSalle Road
Baltimore, Maryland 21204-6020

For more information about the artist, contact:

Charles R. Murphy
True North Studio
518 W. 8th St.
Traverse City, MI 49684

For information about workshops and school
or conference presentations contact:

Hidden Bay Productions
216 West Seventh Street
Traverse City, MI 49684
616-947-2058 or 616-271-3230

Acknowledgments

This book could not have happened without the help and encouragement of many people. Our special thanks to our families: David and Zachary Abeel; Carrie Craig Murphy and David, Jonathan, and Katherine Williams.   Your patience and understanding were always appreciated. We are also indebted to G.F. "Skip" Bourdo, Lana Crandall, Mike Kelly, Dee Massaroni, Dave Millross, Jack Olson, Mary Pratt, Barb Webster and Tom Wilson, without whom this would not be a success story. We deeply appreciate the time and suggestions of the many friends and colleagues who listened to us, encouraged us and helped critique and proofread our manuscript: Dr. Susan K. Baum, Charles and Susan Cady, Corinne Chabot, Laurie Davis, Dr. Donald Deshler, Jerry Dennis, Patricia Dolanski, Cathryn Drewry, Susan Galbraith, Helene Gruber, Jerry Jenkins, Dr. William Lakey, Dr. Mel Levine, Alex Moore, Suzanne Murray, Jim Novak, Chris Okoren, Mary Beth Perkins, Rosie Popa, William Pringle, Mike Romstadt, William Shaw, Connie Sweeny, Susanah Tobin, Dick and Peg Townsend, Barbara VenHorst, Martha Vreeland, A.V. and Emmy Williams, John Robert Williams and Glenn Wolff. Sometimes it was only your enthusiasm that kept us going. A special thank you to Tom Woodruff for helping us to navigate new and unfamiliar waters.